101 Tips and Advice for Life

Tony S. Hilanto

AuthorHouse™
1663 Liberty Drive
Bloomington, IN 47403
www.authorhouse.com
Phone: 833-262-8899

Because of the dynamic nature of the Internet, any web addresses or links contained in this book may have changed since publication and may no longer be valid. The views expressed in this work are solely those of the author and do not necessarily reflect the views of the publisher, and the publisher hereby disclaims any responsibility for them.

Any people depicted in stock imagery provided by Getty Images are models, and such images are being used for illustrative purposes only. Certain stock imagery © Getty Images.

This book is printed on acid-free paper.

ISBN: 978-1-4389-2565-3 (sc)

Print information available on the last page.

Published by AuthorHouse 05/25/2022

authorHOUSE®

Dedication

I dedicate this book to my father, S. P. Hilanto, who started my life journey.

I also dedicate this book to my children and lovely wife for their support and encouragement.

Introduction

For years, I have always wanted to write a simple, easy to understand book filled with advice for others. A few years ago, I was transferred out of state as a cultural advisor for the U.S. Army. It was there I had some time on my hands to write.

My goal for this book is to save people from making many mistakes in their lives, large or small, as we journey through this life. I trust that taking the advice found between these pages will save you from some of the frustrations and stumblings in life.

My hope is that these pieces of advice will help equip you in making wise decisions as you walk through your daily life.

I hope you will enjoy this book, and it becomes a tool of reference on numerous occasions as you see the value of this handbook.

Enjoy life's journey!

Tony S. Hilanto

Contents

The Most Important Advice For Everyone   2

Teenagers   3

Relationships   9

Parenting   11

Cars   13

Kitchen   14

About Life   15

General Advice   16

Other materials available through the author:

The Ultimate Punishment
Two Videos on customer service management and employees (Seminar title: "Customer Service is the Bottom Line)
Reminding Pillowcases
MVB Sportswear (most valuable baby sports wear)

The Most Important Advice For Everyone

Learn how to say the small powerful word "NO."
Learn to say "NO" to strangers.
Learn to say "NO" before signing any contract you do not feel good about.
Learn to say "NO" to a persistent stranger.

Learning how to say "NO" could even save your life. In my lifetime, I have encountered multiple opportunities to exercise a "NO" in my own life. After realizing the consequences I would have had to encounter if I had said "Yes," I can attest that it has saved my life.

Definitely say "NO" to drugs. Drugs will always smoke the smartness out of your brain.

Always say "NO" with confidence.

Teenagers

Teenage years are the most wonderful, most dangerous and the most important stage of our lives. When a person becomes a teenager, he becomes a "teen-eager," eager to know and experience new things in life, and that is where it gets dangerous.

Your looks, voice and growth will all change and the hormones will go crazy. Your brain will become a whole arcade sometimes playing tricks on you and that is how it will get you in trouble. People expect teenagers to act obnoxiously, to not take the opinion of others seriously even if you prove them wrong!

As a teen, you will think you are always right and nobody else knows better than you. You will think everybody wants the worst for you, especially your parents. That is not true. Parents are more careful and concerned than you think about you at that stage of your life.

Instead of looking at going to school as a burden, look at it as a place where you meet friends, can socialize and as you sit in the classroom a teacher is feeding you information. You have to go to school, and that is why you do not like it. But consider this. Even if you had to visit Disneyland every day, you would tire of it. It is like the two things people hate to do. They have to go grocery shopping and put gas in their cars. They hate these tasks because they have to and not because they want to.

Life has its bitter as well as its sweet moments. Replace the bitter moments with the sweet!

Though we will miss our teenage years, we must be sure that we learn from our mistakes and take the advice of others or we may pay for some of them the rest of our lives. We will regret the wrong things we did, but we will be proud of surviving it safely, educationally and successfully because this is

the time that will determine our future.
So enjoy it while it lasts, but do not blow it.

Some advice for teens:

1. Get a hold of your future, before your future gets a hold of you and it throws you somewhere you will not be happy.

2. Your schoolbook is your best friend in life. It will never change on you or betray you; the knowledge will always remain a treasure in your brain. A good college degree is your weapon for life.
So is a good profession.

3. When you are about to do something that is making you hesitate, ask yourself, "Is it better and safer if I do it or not?"

4. Always take what is guaranteed in life, even the simplest things. For example, if you have tentative plans for next Friday and Saturday, but later on you get a confirmed plan for Friday only, take the Friday one. Do the same with jobs and other opportunities.

5. Be a good example for all those who are younger than you including your siblings.

6. As much as you think that you are right as a teenager and refuse to take advice, later on when you grow older, you will regret those moments a hundred times over for not listening.

7. Be good to your parents before it is too late. Do not take for granted the fact that your parents are healthy and alive. Life is full of surprises.

8. Know what you want from life and set a goal; if you think it is too soon; you will be surprised how time flies. Just look how far a month from now is and look how quickly the past five years have gone!

9. Do not prejudge people before you get to know them. If you hate people for whatever reason, get those negative thoughts out of your head. All it will do is frustrates you and shorten your health and life.

10. The secret to happiness is to always think about the things you have and not the things you do not have.

11. Do not drive recklessly or drunk, because if you hit a child and hurt his family, that will be a burden you will carry for the rest of your life.

12. Write your problems on a sheet of paper and you will be surprised how silly they are. This exercise will ease your mind.

13. Do not try to impress your friends by doing something stupid, he will NOT GO TO JAIL FOR YOU OR WITH YOU, he will simply deny having intimidated you.

14. Making the right choices causing you to be different than your friends and classmates, THAT IS WHAT I CALL BEING REALLY COOL! Do not spend all your time studying or playing sport or partying, but balance and divide your time appropriately.

15. When you are stopped by the police, remain calm and cooperative. Do not be a wise guy because they are expecting you to be. Believe me, you will be surprised how cooperative police can be.

16. Live bravely, but not crazily. Live carefully but not like a chicken. Do not be afraid of taking a risk especially after studying all its advantages and disadvantages.

17.   Do not answer yes to something you are not sure you understand. Asking them to repeat it, for a repeat is better than giving a stupid or wrong response. Listen with your ears and do not respond with the first thing that comes into your head.

18. Do not become jealous of someone else, but prove that you can be better (honestly and fairly).

19. Life is like trying to swim in the ocean. The waves keep on throwing you backwards to start over, but you keep on jumping over those obstacles.

20. Life is like a garden. Sometimes the seeds you plant (plan) do not grow only plants! We also get weeds we do not plant (plan).

21. When you are getting a streak of bad days, pull yourself up and out of the problem mentally and live above life.

22. The secret to success is being PATIENT.

23. Do not get intimidated or discouraged by the point of view or the opinion of others; find out the facts before making a change.

24. Do not give up on life so quickly; enjoy the journey and remember, suicide is a permanent solution for a temporary problem.
Just imagine if you committed suicide then you realize that you made a big mistake and you try to get back into life but you cannot.
It is like being behind bars. And drugs are just a temporary escape.

25. Do not become jealous or mad at those who do not need to work but you have to. Believe me, they feel a lack in their life and they envy you for being so independent. In addition, you need the practice for life.

26. Do not bully others, pick on them or degrade them. You never know how high the consequences might be, and it will be unfair if innocent ones pay the price.

27. Think of the future as the Super Bowl and you in training for it.

28. Friends you are going to need in your life: A good lawyer, a good doctor, a good dentist, a good accountant, a good mechanic, a good plumber and a good hairdresser, so work on picking your friends from now on.

29. Everybody is good at some things and weak in other things. That does not mean the things you are weak at makes you ignorant, and not all jobs are for everybody.

30. For everything fun or positive you do, there is a negative for it. For example, when you go to a party you will make new friends, drink, eat, and dance. The down side is somebody might spill their drink on you by accident, somebody might slip you something in your drink, you might get drunk and drive drunk and get a ticket or have an accident! Do not forget that any stain on your record will hunt you for years to come if not for life.

Enjoy life's journey.

Relationships

What is a good relationship? A good relationship is when the foundations of trust and faithfulness are agreed upon.
Remember the three C's:
 a) Communicate
 b) Compromise and
 c) Commitment

In a bad moment, remember that no two people are alike in looks or personality. So always make room for others by forgiving, letting things go and not giving others the 3rd degree. Bite your tongue at that mad moment.

Advice on how to have a good relationship:

1. If you are getting into a relationship with somebody different than your nationality or religion, do your research on the background of that country or religion before you fall too far. Just remember how much background information banks ask for when you are committing to a loan or acquiring a credit card. Don't you think that your life is more valuable? Do your search first.

2. Write down the things that you definitely cannot put up with before you commit to a relationship. Exchange this information with them. This may sound funny, but it is always a good idea to know their credit score.

3. Do not jump the gun if you are mad at your husband or wife and start yelling and fighting as soon as your mate arrives home. Wait few minutes so they can unwind and then ask questions.

4. Gentlemen: If you think that you are smarter than your wife, why do you get mad and yell at her when she makes a mistake!?

5. Ladies: A loud woman usually will make the husband make bad decisions and lose his temper in front of the children. Also, it will affect your children's point of view regarding marriage.

6. A loud husband and father in the house is not a good example for the children; they may copy that personality. You want to be respected more than feared.

7. If the person you are in love with has difficulty making a commitment to you, do not put an extra load on them by rushing them into a decision. It is not going to work out. And even if it does, it will not last long. Be patient.

Parenting

Does it complete our masculinity and femininity by becoming a parent or is it a new beginning and responsibility for us? Is parenting the most important stage in our lives? We are adding more to our generation. How were we prepared financially, physically, patiently, lovingly and educationally to become parents? It is a lifetime commitment.

Some advice to parents:

1. When you are discussing something serious with your kids, either get down to their level or raise them to your eye level contact.

2. For the safety of your children, always put them in the car first and ask if all are in before you back up down the driveway.

3. Always tell your kids how proud you are of them, talk to them about anything, especially right after school when you are picking them up. This will show them that you care about their day at school.

4. Have a bi-weekly or monthly family meeting to discuss what you as well as they are happy or unhappy about.

5. Be kind to your children and thank God for the blessings they are to you. Remember, you are the physical father for them, but after you are gone, God is their father, and He will be wherever they will be.

6. Do not discuss or yell at your children while they are eating especially right after school. Do not let them go to bed unhappy; it is unhealthy.

7. Always put the raw meat at the bottom of the fridge just in case the meat leaks from its packaging. Keep a hand sanitizer in the kitchen especially if you have a baby in the house.

8. Become a friend to your children, but also keep a respectful distance. Discuss things with them so they are comfortable being honest with you. Be sure not accuse them right away. That way they will not hide anything from you or do things behind your back.

9. Since printing a sheet of paper is so available these days, print sayings to your kids such as, "I am so proud of you" or "Make me proud", etc. Hang it in their bedroom.

10. After using the restroom, clean underneath your nails too because babies like to suck on fingers.

11. If you are traveling with a child or going to a crowded place, make a name tag with your address or hotel address on it in case something happens to you. Also, take a picture for your luggage with your cell phone in case they get lost.

12. Do not shake a baby or hurt him, remember he is putting his trust in you.

13. A good punishment is not to speak to your kids after warning them not to do something you did not want them to do.

Cars

In my opinion, the most wonderful invention is the car! It is used for transportation, carrying groceries, sleeping and luxury. I believe it is more valuable than many other inventions.

Tips about cars:

1. If you are buying a used car, it is well worth the check-up fee, especially if you are not mechanically inclined.

2. Tips on how to save gas:

 Before you start up the car, be sure to adjust your mirrors, put your seat belt on, roll down the windows, tune the radio to your preferred station, then start up the engine. And do the same vice-versa. After arriving, time after time, day after day it will add up. Also, the right air pressure in your tires will save you gas. Taking off and stopping quickly will burn more gas, wear the brakes out plus it will hurt the mounts on your engine.

3. When giving a jump-start to somebody's else car, always hook the cables to your running car first; do not let the two cars touch at all. Opposite action will instantly drain out your battery.

4. Always pump your brakes after a car wash or driving through a dip of water to prevent a skid; also pump your brakes before driving into your garage on a rainy day.

5. Every time you leave your car, get into the habit of locking your doors, making sure your headlights are off as well as the inside lights. Treat your car as if you are leaving it for an entire day.

Kitchen

The most important part of the house is the kitchen.
You can get healthy or sick out of your own kitchen.

Some of the tips are:

1. When you are using a knife, always cut away from you and not toward you. Also, if you are using a sharp tool or a screwdriver trying to get something out, always do it away from your face, because you might miss and poke your eye.

2. Always wait at least five seconds after using the microwave before opening the door.

3. When chopping food, tuck your fingers into your palm with thumb inside and slide the knife downward on an angle with the sharp side away from your fingers.

4. Do not try to catch a falling knife off the counter or a table; most likely you will grab the sharp end and cut yourself. If this happens, turn away from the knife and let it fall.

5. If you have the smallest cut on your hand, do not let it touch raw meat or it may get badly infected.

6. The best way to make a sandwich is first to spread the mustard on one side of the bread, lay the cheese on it, then the meat, the tomatoes, the pickles, the lettuce then the mayo on the other side of the bread to stick on the lettuce which acts as a dressing.

About Life

How lucky are you in life? Unfortunately, some people do not know what enough is! Being modest and content is a life's treasure.

Here are some tips for life:

1. If you were born healthy, that is a plus.
If you were born healthy and smart, that is another plus.
If you were born healthy, smart and with a single parent, that is another plus.
If you were born healthy and smart with two parents, that is another plus.
And if you add wealth to that, that is another plus.
That does not mean others are out of luck. Basically, if God has given you all the above which you have no control over, the rest of your life is your challenge.

2. Life is a teaser, so tease it back and do not let it get to you.

3. Know the strategy of your life—when to take action and when not to!
For example, I have noticed the timing in my life that if I wait five minutes before taking any action, it will work out better for me timing-wise.

General Advice

Always be open to good advice. Never be too stubborn to take advice.

1. Do not ever make a decision when you are mad. You might regret it later, so try to control your mouth and your actions.

2. Do not leave home mad and drive.

3. Do not do something that is so bad that it is irreversible, like killing somebody or hurting someone permanently. These are things you will pay for for the rest of your life.

4. Whenever you call a company, always write down the name, extension number and the time you called.

5.   If an offer sounds too good to be true, then it is not true. For example, giving money to somebody claiming that he will double it or more in a very short period of time.

6. Always plan on arriving at least ten minutes early for work; it is far better to sit in the parking lot than the freeway.

7. An easy way not to gain weight is never keep eating until you are full, or eat half of the amount and walk 20 minutes a day.

8. If you are living alone, have a pet or a plant, it will keep your memory warm.

9. If you lost your love or a loved one, and cannot stop thinking about that person, sit and mediate for a minute. Give that person a small place in your heart, leave the memory there and get on with your life. Get involved in sports, hobbies, go out with friends, and watch happy movies.

10. Give a good customer service at your work; your day will go faster and who knows, you might get an offer from a customer for a better opportunity.

11. If you get into a silly problem like gum gets stuck in your hair, guess who to call? Your local library.

12. If you see something strange on the floor of your house and want to pick it up, step on it first then pick it up. It might be a spider or some insect, especially in a new house.

13. Treat people the way you want to be treated. Someday you might need the help of that person.

14. If you are getting impatient with your goals, sit down for a minute, close your eyes and imagine all your dreams coming true at once. I will bet you will feel your life instantly become boring because all of your dreams have come true. (Try it now.) Enjoy the challenge.

15. If you do not speak good English or have an accent, without interrupting, always start your conversation with the magic words "Excuse me" and end it with a "Thank you." It will make things easier for you and you will get the proper service and respect.

16. Every morning start your day with at least one minute of stretching; start with a scalp massage, neck stretch, shoulders, arms, hips, legs, knees and feet. It will make a big difference.
Lie on the floor on your back and extend your arms and legs for 30 seconds. Then, roll over on your side, your front, your other side and end on your back.

17. Be a believer in God; He will organize your life for you. He has the remote control.

18. Do not sign a contract with a long commitment without seeing a lawyer, it is worth the monetary investment. (Better safe than sorry.)

19. Remember, the shortest pencil is better than the longest memory.

20. If you have too much in your head to do for the month or the week, write those things down and see how your head feels lighter.

21. If you are out shopping and saw something you liked but you do not really need it and are short on money that month, don't charge it, but ask yourself: What is it that I can do today to gain that money? In other words, it is easy to go but hard to come back.

22. If you were tired of standing on your feet all day at work, here is a good tip: Lay down on your back on the floor, put your feet up, slide your bottom against the wall with your feet straight up the wall for a minute. Put one of your heels on your big toe for another minute and reverse it. Within minutes, you will see a major difference in your legs.

23. If you are carrying cash, do not put it all in one pocket; distribute it over several pockets. That way, if you lose one you have not lost all the money. This is especially helpful if you are traveling. Never put cash in your wallet with your credit cards because if you lose the wallet you will not get the credit cards back. They will take the cash and leave the wallet.

24. Always carry a camera in your car or use your cell phone camera; in case of an accident, take pictures before cars are moved and definitely take a picture of the license plate, especially on a hit and run.

25. If you are going to gamble, especially out of town and you are tight on money, make sure that you pay all your bills before going. Otherwise, if you come back as a loser with all the bills still waiting for you at the dining table, it will not be a good feeling. Learn how to put up with losing before winning.

26. If you are depressed all the time, see a psychiatrist. It helps just to have a stranger listen to you if you disagree with your family's advice.

27. When walking on a slippery surface (especially going downhill), walk slowly, bend your knees a bit, spread your feet, do not even them out, and lean forward.

28. If you are ever soaping your face in the shower, and soap got into your nose and you cannot breathe, do not panic! Remember, you can always breathe from your mouth.

29. Children should be loved purely. Nothing is worse than robbing the innocence of a child. That child will be marked for life.

30. Whenever you pick up a prescription from a pharmacy, always be sure it is your medicine.

31. When driving, obey the law, so if you ever get into an accident, at least you cannot blame yourself.

32. If you are leasing a new space that needs tenant improvements, find out in writing from what point of construction the landlord will pay the tenant improvement.

33. Whenever I am in a situation where I get nervous or afraid, I ask the Lord Jesus to give me an ounce of His courage, and instantly all the fear and panic disappear.

34. If you ever get attacked, remember to always go for the eyes or the nostrils.

35. Unfortunately, life to lots of people is whoever can outsmart the other. Whether it is at school or work or getting that promotion, some people will sweet talk you or even beg you to get what they want. Be careful of the manipulative ploys of the sweet talker whether it is for money or sex. Remember, if anything goes wrong later on, their reply may be, "I didn't put a gun to your head, did I?"
So be smarter than them, study the situation, and do your research first.

36. Do not jerk heavy items such as pulling a suitcase or moving a couch because you run the risk of tearing a ligament in your elbow. You may not feel it for a few days, but the cure will take months.

37 Brush and floss your teeth before sleeping or at least swish after each meal, and when you brush, brush at an angle between the teeth and the gums.

38. So, you are unappreciative for what you have or you think that life has not been fair to you? How about feeling the problems of others problem temporarily, like blindfolding yourself for a day and going through your regular day feeling the darkness of the blind, or the loneliness of the deaf person?

39. If you have to do something later, then you have the opportunity to do it sooner. Do it, because if you do not you might just forget about it.

40. Before you leave your husband or your wife or the kids, explain to your partner your true feelings and your point of view and how to correct the situation, and then make that big decision.
Again, do not make fast decisions when you angry.

41. Always cross the street horizontally not diagonally; it is the shortest distance and minimizes the opportunity for an accident. When crossing at night, remember the driver can only see as far as his headlights can travel and in the rain, he cannot stop right away. And not everybody has 20/20 vision.

42. So you hate your manager. Just remember he is caught between pleasing his boss and the customers, so think about what you are going to say to him first.

43. If you have not played a sport in a while, stretch out before and after the game so you do not have body aches.

44. So you are rich and have everything, but there is still emptiness in your life. How about doing something for others such as helping the orphans? It is a good, rewarding feeling.

45. Salute all military personnel. You will never appreciate the sacrifices they make unless you work with them.

The author of this book does not guarantee or take any responsibility for any tips or advice that does not work for the reader.

Printed in the United States
by Baker & Taylor Publisher Services